DISCOVER

GOD

BIBLE STUDY NO. 1

Based on the book
DISCOVER GOD
by **Dr. Bill Bright**

Group

Loveland, Colorado
www.group.com

Discover God Bible Study No. 1

Visit our Web site: **www.group.com**

Credits

Authors: Cheri Gillard, Keith Madsen, Carl Simmons, and Jeff White
Project Manager: Scott M. Kinner
Editor: Brad Lewis
General Editors: Brad and Kathy Bright
Copy Editor: Daniel Birks
Senior Developer: Roxanne Wieman
Chief Creative Officer: Joani Schultz
Art Director: Jeff Storm
Book Designer: YaYe Design
Cover Art Designer: Jeff Storm
Print Production Artist: YaYe Design
Production Manager: Peggy Naylor

Library of Congress Cataloging-in-Publication Data

Discover God series : Bible study / Cheri Gillard ... [et al.]. -- 1st American pbk. ed.
     p. cm.
   ISBN 978-0-7644-3556-0 (pbk. : alk. paper) 1. Bright, Bill. God--Textbooks. 2. God (Christianity)--Attributes--Textbooks. I. Gillard, Cheri R. II. Group Publishing.
   BT130.D57 2007
   231'.4071--dc22
                              2007014154

ISBN 978-0-7644-3556-0

10 9 8 7 6 5 4 3 2 1   16 15 14 13 12 11 10 09 08 07

Printed in the United States of America.

FOREWORD

The key to the joyful Christian life is having a clear understanding of who God *really* is.

It's not about me. I cannot fix myself. No one else can fix me. (My wife will attest to that.) Only God can. Even my ability to have faith and believe God for great things is nothing more than a mere symptom of my view of God.

Too often our view of God is bent or incomplete, and we don't even know it. Sometimes we water down His sovereignty by unwittingly taking partial credit for what God did. Other times we focus on His love but forget that He is also holy, which blocks us from fully experiencing the incredible depth of His love.

My father, Bill Bright, said, "We can trace all of our human problems to our view of God." What we believe to be true about God's character affects *every* aspect of our lives. God, and God alone, is the issue.

I watched my dad build Campus Crusade for Christ into a worldwide organization of 26,000 full-time staff and 250,000 trained volunteers. With calm assurance he navigated monumental decisions that sometimes had life-and-death implications. I watched him cultivate a marriage that was strong, full of laughter, and deep with love. I saw him passionately pursue a vital relationship with the living God up until his dying breath. I was there. And the key to it all was his radically expansive view of God.

That lesson was not lost on me, his son. This Bible study is the direct result of our prayer that this lesson will not be lost on you either.

Apart from death and taxes, there is one thing you can count on—your life will be powerfully transformed as you come to better understand who God *really* is.

Yours for making *God* the issue,

Brad Bright
National Director, Discover God
President & CEO, Bright Media Foundation

P.S. If you would like additional information about *Discover God*, please visit us at www.DiscoverGod.com.

CONTENTS

DISCOVER GOD SERIES, NO. 1

Just a few years before he died at age 81 from complications related to pulmonary fibrosis, a degenerative disease of the lungs, Campus Crusade for Christ founder Bill Bright published a remarkable book titled *God: Discover His Character* (now titled *Discover God*). This book was remarkable because it boldly attempted to help Christians understand and know who God is, what He's like, and why or how He does what he does. We often call these qualities the *attributes* of God. They describe His character and very nature.

The study you're holding now takes Bill Bright's exploration of six of God's attributes and helps you understand and experience them in your own life. But you might be wondering, "If those qualities belong to God, can I really experience any of His character in my life?"

Good question. And the answer is yes. God's ultimate plan is an intimate relationship with us. If we have the correct view of His character, we can more easily relate to Him— and that's exactly what He desires!

So, that's the goal of this study: to help you grasp a right view of God's character, to improve and grow your relationship with God, and to help you adopt God's character so that it emanates back out of your life.

Here's how this study works:

First, the study is meant to be done in a group setting—this might be a Sunday school class or a small group that meets in a home. Everyone in your group will participate in learning about God's attributes by taking part in hands-on activities.

At first, these activities might seem . . . well . . . different. Remember, though, that Jesus often used everyday items to make His message more real to His listeners. For example, His disciples were certainly uncomfortable and even a bit confused when He washed their feet (John 13:5-17). Jesus had to reassure them, "You do not realize now what I am doing, but later you will understand" (verse 7, NIV). Yet this turned out to be a powerful lesson that stayed with them the rest of their lives. The goal is for your group to have a similar experience as you do the activities in these sessions. You'll learn God's eternal truth in brand-new ways—and have fun in the process!

Your group will also dig into relevant Bible passages and discuss thought-provoking questions that will help you understand how the attribute you're examining applies to your own lives.

In addition, each session concludes with opportunities to help you live out that attribute of God in your own life. As you put the ideas into practice throughout each week, you'll discover God deepening your understanding of His character in your relationship with Him, with yourself, and with others.

So, welcome to Discover God! The team who put together these books prays that you'll find the studies and experiences both meaningful and memorable. As you do the sessions together, may your lives increasingly reflect and show the qualities and character of God.

—*Brad Lewis, Editor*

▶ About the Sessions

Each participant should have his or her own copy of the
Discover God Bible Study for content that everyone will use.
Throughout the sessions, you'll also find hints for leaders
and subgroup leaders.

Briefly, here's how each session breaks down:

▶ Warm Up and Tune In (10 minutes)

You'll start by taking a few minutes to introduce yourselves
to any new members in your class or group. In addition,
you'll do an activity that helps you get to know each other
better and helps you tune in to the attribute you'll be
studying in the session.

At the end of this section of each session, you'll also find
a helpful hint called "God Is Personal"—which provides
you with insight on how you can make God's attribute a
personal and intimate part of your life.

▶ Dig and Discover (40 minutes)

This is the central part of what your group will do together. You'll study some Bible passages related to the
attribute you're learning about, as well as interact with each
other as you talk through some challenging questions, read
what Bill Bright and others have to say about the attribute,
and participate in some sensory experiences to solidify the
ways God's attribute applies to your life.

▶ Reflect and Respond (15 minutes)

Now you'll make things even more personal. You'll continue to wrestle with knowing more about God's character,
and you'll consider how you might respond to God in the
area of that attribute.

▶ Making It Real (25 minutes)

In this part of the session, you'll choose a weekly challenge that will help you make God's attribute a part of your life in a practical way. You'll also share prayer requests with your group, pray for each other, and make plans to connect with another group member before the next session, just to check in and encourage one another.

▶ This Coming Week

This final section provides some important reminders as you go throughout the coming week: It prompts you to check in with someone else in your group during the week, urges you to write down a response to God's attribute that you'll work on in the coming week, and provides you with a list of Bible passages for further study.

BECAUSE GOD IS
ALL-POWERFUL,
He can help me with anything.

"He does not derive His power from any other source; all power has always been His and will continue to be His for eternity. Any power that we have comes ultimately from God."

—Bill Bright, Discover God

▶ For this session, you'll need...

■ An uninflated balloon for each group member

■ At least one straight-back or folding chair for each subgroup of three or four people

Sunday school teachers:
If you're using this study for a class rather than a small group, consider starting with the "Dig and Discover" section (beginning on page 12) to help your class stay within its time limits. (If you choose to skip the "Warm Up and Tune In" section, you won't need the uninflated balloons from the supply list above.)

▶ Warm Up and Tune In (10 minutes)

If this is your first time together as a group, take a few minutes to introduce yourselves to one another.

Once you've gotten to know each other a little better, stand up and line up side by side, all facing the same direction. Make sure you have several feet of space in front of your line.

Leader: Give an uninflated balloon to each group member.

When your leader says "go," throw the uninflated balloon as far as you can in front of you.

Pick up your balloon. This time, blow it up, but don't tie

it. Line up again with the other group members, and aim your balloon in front of you. Wait again for your leader to say "go," and then let it go!

Find your balloon—if you can! Then sit back down and discuss the following questions:

■ What were some differences between how the balloon traveled each time? What made the difference in each case?

■ Can you see any ways that this is like the difference between trying to do things under our own power versus doing them by *God's* power?

■ Can you think of a time during the past week where *you* could have used a little more "inflating" to get by? How would it have helped?

$\mathcal{G}$OD IS PERSONAL: All-Powerful

Just how powerful *is* God? Read Genesis 15:1-6 and 21:1-5 on your own time, and discover how God created life in a most improbable situation. God also brought joy into the lives of a husband and wife who waited a long time for the son God promised them.

For an even greater example of God's power to create life—and of His love for each one of us—check out Luke 1:28-38!

"$\mathcal{G}$od is capable of doing anything—as long as it does not violate His other attributes. (For example, He cannot lie, change, deny himself or be tempted.) Otherwise, no task is too large or too difficult for Him. He never fails or gets tired."

—Bill Bright, Discover God

▶ **Dig and Discover** (40 minutes)

■ What do you think it means that God is all-powerful?

Jeremiah 32:17 says, "O Sovereign Lord! You made the heavens and earth by your strong hand and powerful arm. Nothing is too hard for you!" As you think about this verse, answer the following questions:

■ What do you think this verse reveals about God's power?

■ Do you think most people really believe this is true? Why or why not?

Now read Ephesians 3:14–21, and answer the following questions:

■ Look again at verses 14–16. What do these verses reveal about God and His power? What do they reveal about how God uses His power?

■ How does Paul respond to God's all-powerfulness here? In your life, how do you respond to God's power?

■ What does Paul pray for the Ephesians in this passage? How does understanding God's love lead to life and power?

■ Why do you think it's important for God to "empower *you* with inner strength through his Spirit"? How would your life be changed if you had the kind of strength Paul prays for here?

■ Have you experienced God's power in your life like Paul did? If so, what did it look like and how did it affect your relationship with God? Yourself? Others?

Now, break into subgroups.

Leader: To help increase your group's participation, break into smaller subgroups of three or four. Make sure each subgroup has at least one straight-back or folding chair. You can ask for volunteers to serve as subgroup leaders, or you can recruit individuals before your class or group meets.

Subgroup leaders: Find a place where your subgroup can talk with few distractions. Plan to come back together in 25 minutes.

Every small group is different. Your timing is different. The way you answer questions is different. Your group dynamic is different. All that to say, you're going to go through this study in a different way than another group will. Which means—as the leader—it's smart to read through the study ahead of time. Pick out questions that are relevant to your group. Hopefully, you'll have time to get through all the questions, but you might want to linger on some and skip others…and that's OK! Tailor the study as needed for your group time, and encourage your small group members to answer any skipped questions on their own during the week.

You really can experience God's power in your life! To learn more, go to www.DiscoverGod.com.

▶ Activity

Break your subgroups into pairs. If you have two chairs for each subgroup, have one partner sit and the other stand; if not, let each pair take a turn doing this activity.

Instruct one partner to sit down with arms crossed across the chest, and then ask the seated partners to try to stand up. Here's the catch: Before the seated partner attempts to stand, the standing partner will place a finger on the seated partner's forehead and push gently.

Have partners reverse positions. After everyone takes a turn sitting, discuss the following:

■ What happened as each person attempted to stand? What was it like to be the seated person? The standing one?

■ Think about a recent situation where you felt powerless. In what ways was it like the activity you just did? What was hardest about that situation?

"The sun, with all the planets revolving around it and depending on it can still ripen a bunch of grapes as though it had nothing else in the universe to do. Why then should I doubt His power?"

—Galileo Galilei

Now, read Mark 4:35-41 in your subgroups, and discuss the following questions:

■ What two questions do the disciples ask in this passage (see verses 38 and 41)? What do you think the first question says about the disciples' relationship with Jesus? Why do you think they asked these questions?

■ Have you ever been in a difficult or frightening situation and wondered if God cared about you? Describe that situation.

■ Have you ever felt that someone or something had so much power over you that even God couldn't help you?

"I can do everything through Christ, who gives me strength"

(Philippians 4:13)

■ What do your answers to these questions tell you about your *own* ability to trust in God's power? Explain.

To hear others discuss how they've experienced God's power, go to www.DiscoverGod.com.

■ Look at the list to the right. Does one or more of those words (or others) represent a storm in your life right now where you need God's power? How would your attitude change in this situation if you could be completely confident of God's power?

Come back together as a larger group, and share any highlights or questions from your subgroup discussion.

"The worshiping man finds this knowledge a source of wonderful strength for his inner life. His faith rises to take the great leap upward into the fellowship of Him who can do whatever He wills to do, for whom nothing is hard or difficult because He possesses power absolute."

—A. W. Tozer

"Since nothing is too hard for God, we do not have a need too great for Him to meet nor a problem too complicated for Him to conquer. We can never pray a prayer too difficult for Him to answer."

—Bill Bright, Discover God

Addiction
Broken relationships
Hopelessness
Jealousy
Critical attitude
Poor self-image
Conflict
Depression
Failure
Bad habits
Unexpected illness
Financial troubles
Stress
Sexual temptations
Unemployment
Anxiety
Transitions
Apathy
Bitterness
Disappointment
Fear
Panic
Suffering
Tension
Dissatisfaction
Vulnerable
Worry
Anger
Hatred
Questioning God
Resentment
Self-centeredness
Trials
Unhappiness

▶ Reflect and Respond (15 minutes)

Read Matthew 7:7-11. Then discuss the following:

■ What's one "fish"—a desire of your heart—that you're waiting for God to provide right now? On a scale from 1 to 10, how confident are you in God's power for that situation (10 being "There's a truckload of fish coming my way"; 1 being "I'll be lucky if I get a goldfish in a baggie")? Why?

■ How would a deeper understanding that God really *is* all-powerful—and cares for you—change the way you're looking at, and responding to, that situation? Explain.

" *I*f we really believe that God is all-powerful, we will no longer walk in fear and unbelief. We will place our faith in God—not necessarily great faith in God, but rather faith in a great God who is omnipotent. In turn, He will lead us into a life full of adventure and purpose. I have found no better way to live!"

— *Bill Bright*, Discover God

■ What would help you to catch more of God's power right now? What could your group do to help you know and trust more in the all-powerfulness of God?

■ How would catching more of God's power give you hope this week?

▶ Making It Real (25 minutes)

Break into pairs.

The options below can help you make God's power a part of your *own* life as you put the ideas into practice. Select the option you'd like to take on this week, and share your choice with your partner. Then make plans to connect sometime between now and the next session to check in and encourage each other.

☐ **OPTION 1: Praise God.** Set aside a block of time this week (at least 30 minutes) to reflect on the completeness of God's power and to praise Him simply for who He is. Read all of Psalm 19 or other Bible passages such as Psalm 104, Isaiah 40:28-31, or Philippians 4:12-13. Spend some time in prayer, inviting God to become more involved *in* your life and asking how He wants His power to shine *through* your life.

☐ **OPTION 2: Let God work—and watch the results.** Is there an area of your life where you've been feeling powerless? Resolve to surrender that situation to God each day this week. Keep a journal during the week, reflecting on how God has worked in those circumstances and how He's guided you through them. As you begin to see victory in that area, talk to someone else about how God's power is working in your life.

☐ **OPTION 3: Share the power.** Think about how God's power has already brought positive change in your life. Then ask God to bring to mind someone else who's facing similar circumstances. How can you share what God's power has done for you, as well as offer encouragement and support to that person? Commit to calling him or her this week and setting up a time to meet.

☐ **OPTION 4: Have a "power out–age."** Who are the "powerless" in your community, those who really need to see God's power and love? Together, identify one such group and come up with a plan for helping them. Pray for God's guidance concerning how He wants you to get involved. Consider your passions, your availability, and your location. Work together to identify a practical, meaningful way you can help, and then get to it!

☐ **OPTION 5: Find out what others think.** Ask two or three friends to join you for coffee or pizza this week. Ask a few questions about what they think of God's power. For example, do they think that God's power is infinite or limited and why? Have they ever experienced God's power in their life? Do they have an area in their life they struggle with—one where God's power could make a real difference? Be creative! But, of course, don't critique their opinions. Instead, you might want to relate an area where God's power has made a difference in your life or share something you learned from this session. Don't get preachy. The point is to get them to start asking themselves the right questions.

" I am the vine; you are the branches. Those who remain in me, and I in them, will produce much fruit. For apart from me you can do nothing"

(John 15:5).

▶ Prayer

Come back together as a group. Share your prayer requests. Before the leader prays, take a few moments to be silent and appreciate that God *is* all-powerful and that He wants to use His power in every area of your life. Spend time surrendering to God those areas of your life where you've been running on your own power so that instead, His power can shine through.

▶ This Coming Week

1. Fill in the following: My response to God's Mighty Power this week will be to:

_____

_____

_____

_____

2. Touch base sometime before the next session with your weekly challenge partner to compare notes on how you're both doing with the goals you've set.

3. To learn more about God's Mighty Power read the section in Bill Bright's *Discover God*, on *God Is All-Powerful*. If you don't have a copy of the book, you can find it online to download and print out for free. Just go to www.DiscoverGod.com.

4. If you'd like to discover and connect with God even more deeply each day throughout the coming week, visit www.DiscoverGod.com.

To discover more about God's Mighty Power, start your journey on page 2141 of the Discover God Bible.

BECAUSE GOD IS
HOLY,

I will devote myself to Him in purity, worship, and service.

"Of all God's attributes, nothing compares to the splendor and beauty of His holiness. It is chief among His attributes. That means His character is perfect in every way. He is totally pure."

—Bill Bright, Discover God

▶ For this session, you'll need...

■ A clear drinking glass for each person—crystal glasses if you have them

■ Purified and slightly chilled drinking water in a glass bottle (not plastic) for each subgroup

■ Some offensive-tasting items: sour milk, rotting or spoiled food, or dirt. Be creative!

■ Small spoons, stir sticks, or Q-tips

Sunday school teachers:
If you're using this study for a class rather than a small group, consider starting with the "Dig and Discover" section (beginning on page 23) to help your class stay within its time limits.

▶ Warm Up and Tune In (10 minutes)

Gather into groups of about three or four. If you don't know each other, be sure to introduce yourselves to one another.

Leader: You might want to provide scrap paper and pens during this portion of the study for the groups to take notes as they plan their reception.

In your group, plan a reception for someone of notable standing, such as the queen of England, the president, a respected celebrity, or any other individual your group chooses to represent a person of high regard.

Take about five minutes to determine how you would honor this person, such as with a ticker tape parade, a banquet or reception, entertainment, or an award presentation. Think about how you'd dress and how you'd behave in the notable person's presence.

Once you've determined how you'd honor this person, take a few minutes to discuss the following questions:

■ Why do we honor esteemed personalities? What does it do for us? For the person being honored?

■ How do you feel about honoring a select individual?

■ How is giving honor to a celebrity similar to approaching God with honor?

■ Compare how you'd respond if God came to your home with how you'd react in the presence of a worldly monarch or movie star. What are the similarities? The differences?

■ What are some ways you honor God?

GOD IS PERSONAL: Holy

Consider Jesus and His holiness. The Bible teaches that all that we find in God we also find in Jesus. Since God is holy, Jesus, who is God, is also holy. And Jesus left His throne—where angels cry out around Him, "Holy, holy, holy!"—and came to earth, taking on the limitation and ordinary nature of humanity, for *us*. To *save* us. Now *that* is a personal God!

Take some time this week to read John 1:1-18 and consider anew who Jesus is and what He has done for you!

▶ Dig and Discover (40 minutes)

■ When you think of God's holiness, what comes to mind?

■ Read again Bill Bright's quote at the beginning of the chapter. Why do you think he referred to God's holiness as chief among God's attributes?

Read Isaiah 6:1-5 and 1 John 1:5. Then answer the following questions:

■ What was your reaction as you read Isaiah 6:1-5? How do these verses affect your perception of God?

■ In what ways does God's holiness make you uncomfortable?

■ Describe what you think God would be like if He weren't holy. What makes you think that?

■ Read 1 John 1:5 again. Do you find comfort in the truth that "God is light, and there is no darkness in him"?

Now, read Isaiah 64:6, Luke 18:9-14, and John 3:20-21, and answer the following questions:

■ What do these verses show you about the state of humanity and its relationship to God? What about your own relationship to him?

■ What do you grasp from these passages about approaching God?

■ How do you think people today can truly experience God's holiness? Describe a time you experienced His holiness. How did that experience change your relationship with God?

"No matter how…good we may try to be, we cannot expect God to allow us into His heaven when we have sin stains in our lives. If He allowed one sin to mar His pure dwelling place, it would cease to be a holy city."

—Bill Bright, Discover God

You really can experience God's holiness in your life! To learn more, go to www.DiscoverGod.com.

Now, break into subgroups.

Leader: To help increase your group's participation, break into smaller subgroups of three or four. Make sure each subgroup has sour milk, rotting or spoiled food, dirt, and a glass bottle of pure water, along with enough crystal or clear glasses for each person. You can ask for volunteers to serve as subgroup leaders, or you can recruit individuals before your class or group meets.

Subgroup leaders: Find a place where your subgroup can enjoy a discussion without distractions. Plan to rejoin the larger group in 30 minutes.

▶ Activity

Open the glass bottle of purified water, and pour some into each subgroup member's crystal glass. Ask group members to slowly drink some of their water, savoring it as they do.

Now have subgroup members place their glasses down where the subgroup leader can reach them. The leader should open a container with the sour milk, rotting or spoiled food, or dirt and place a small amount in each person's glass. Now ask who would like to take another slow sip of water, savoring it as they drink.

Now discuss the following:

■ How is the glass of water like God?

■ How did even a small amount of an impure or spoiled substance affect the pure water?

■ What do you think this teaches us about sin from God's perspective—even when we sin in a small way, such as a "little white lie"?

" Only God is holy, just as only people are human. God's holiness is His Godness. To speak of anything else as holy is to say that it has something of God's mark upon it."

—Frederick Buechner,
Wishful Thinking

■ With this activity in mind, why do you think sin is so destructive to our relationship with God?

■ How do you think this might affect the way you approach God?

In your subgroups, read the following passages and discuss these questions:

■ Read 1 Peter 1:15-16. What expectation does God have of us?

■ Read Hebrews 10:10-19. What is God's role?

■ Read 1 John 1:9, Ephesians 5:18, and Psalm 96:9. What is our role in response to God?

■ What do these passages tell us about God's holiness and how we—as His people—should respond to His holiness?

■ This week, in your own life, how can you respond to God's holiness in a new way?

"I am the light of the world. If you follow me, you won't have to walk in darkness, because you will have the light that leads to life" (John 8:12).

■ Look at the list to the right. Does one or more of those words (or others) represent an area in your life right now where you need to submit to God's holiness? How would your attitude change in this situation if you could be completely confident that God is holy and can give you the power to become holy? How might your life look different if you really embraced God's holiness?

To hear others discuss how they've experienced God's holiness, go to www.DiscoverGod.com.

Addiction
Broken relationships
Hopelessness
Jealousy
Critical attitude
Poor self-image
Conflict
Depression
Failure
Bad habits
Unexpected illness
Financial troubles
Stress
Sexual temptations
Unemployment
Anxiety
Transitions
Apathy
Bitterness
Disappointment
Fear
Panic
Suffering
Tension
Dissatisfaction
Vulnerable
Worry
Anger
Hatred
Questioning God
Resentment
Self-centeredness
Trials
Unhappiness

Come back together as a larger group, and share any highlights or questions from your subgroup discussion.

"*The* pursuit of holiness is a joint venture between God and the Christian. No one can attain any degree of holiness without God working in his life, but just as surely no one will attain it without effort on his own part."

—Jerry Bridges, The Pursuit of Holiness

"*As* the holiness of God is absorbed into every fiber of our being, we become even more sensitive to sin and learn to abhor it all the more as we walk in an intimate, joyful relationship with Him."

—Bill Bright, Discover God

▶ **Reflect and Respond** (15 minutes)

Read Romans 11:33–12:2. Then discuss the following:

■ These verses describe how God is set apart—how He is holy—and unlike any other being. He is beyond our comprehension. How does this passage describe the way God wants you to respond to Him? Be specific, applying this to your own life.

■ What in your life needs to change to make you a holy and pleasing living sacrifice to God?

■ How does having a deeper understanding of God's holiness affect your worship? How will you worship God differently this week based on this knowledge?

"*Holy*, righteous living is the secret to a life of joy, power, victory, and fruitfulness. When we are holy, we are set apart and separated for God's special use. God gives us the power to experience a whole new life based on His holiness and purity."

—Bill Bright, Discover God

■ As a Christian, you've been cleansed and made holy in God's sight. How has that changed the course of your life?

■ How would experiencing more of God's holiness give you hope this week?

Sunday school teachers: *If you have time, break your class into pairs and ask them to do the "Making It Real" section that follows. As your class ends, encourage the pairs to pray together for each other. By doing this in class, the extra accountability will help participants follow through on the assignments they choose. Urge the pairs to touch base during the week—as a weekly challenge partner—to encourage each other and compare notes.*

If you're out of time, assign this section to your class as homework. It's an opportunity to make God's holiness come alive in very real and practical ways.

GOD'S CHARACTER IN CONTEXT

Session 1 focused on God's power: "Because God is all-powerful, He can help me with anything." This session focused on God's holiness: "Because God is holy, I will devote myself to Him in purity, worship, and service."

How do you think God can demonstrate His power in your life yet still remain holy and pure?

▶ Making It Real (25 minutes)

Break into pairs.

The options below can help you experience God's power in your *own* life as you put the ideas into practice. Select the option you'd like to take on this week, and share your choice with your partner. Then make plans to connect sometime between now and the next session to check in and encourage each other.

☐ **OPTION 1: Living sacrifice.** Determine a way you can honor God and His holiness through an act of your own holiness. How can you exemplify holiness in a new way? Pray and ask God to show you how He would have you live out your spiritual act of worship through some action. Perhaps you can do an act of service for someone in need. Or maybe you can give up something or take on something new. Consider what He might be calling you to do, and explore how to accomplish it. Then do it!

☐ **OPTION 2: Worship.** Take some time to come before God and acknowledge His holiness. Take a walk, sit on a park bench, or head off to a quiet room. Just be alone with God. Speak and sing out loud. Use phrases that begin with "You are…" Avoid requests or complaints, and even thanksgiving, in order to dedicate the time to telling God what you recognize of His magnificence and holiness. Read Isaiah 6:1-5 and sing or read the words to the hymn "Holy, Holy, Holy" or a praise chorus that honors His name. Give God at least a half-hour of your time, using it just to offer Him praise and worship.

☐ **OPTION 3: Set apart for God.** Take a piece of paper and list specific ways you've chosen to set apart your life for God, such as tithing, serving at church or in your community, praying with your family, and so forth. How do you choose to be holy? When you've finished, look over your list. Ask God to guide you as you consider your life and explore new or different ways He wants you to be set apart for Him. Invite someone from the group or a trusted friend to do this with you, and then encourage each other and pray for each other.

☐ **OPTION 4: Be holy.** Part of being holy is spending time and energy on sharing the good news of Jesus Christ. Is there a person you have a relationship with who isn't a believer, who is ready to hear the reason for your hope in Jesus? Take time to pray and consider how you can intentionally share your personal experience of knowing Jesus with your friend. Consider appropriate questions you might pose so that you can comfortably and sincerely tell your friend about your relationship with God and ask your friend about his or her thoughts and ideas. Remember: You don't have to convince anyone of anything—that's the work of the Holy Spirit. Simply pray for your friend and yourself in preparation for your time together, and then simply take the chance God provides to talk about Jesus.

☐ **OPTION 5: Spiritual audit.** Does a sin in your life continue to hold you in bondage, making you feel anything but holy? Or maybe one area of your life is continually a struggle but you're not sure why. You just know something isn't right. Allow the Holy Spirit to search your heart and tell you, revealing to you the truth God wants you to know. Ask a trusted friend to pray with you as you go about the process of allowing God's Spirit to work. Then ask the Lord to search your heart and reveal to you insight, hope, conviction, or anything else He wishes. Read Psalm 139 during your prayer time, and trust the holy and loving Lord to show you His truth.

"I am the vine; you are the branches. Those who remain in me, and I in them, will produce much fruit. For apart from me you can do nothing"

(John 15:5).

▶ Prayer

Come back together as a group. Share your prayer requests. Before the leader prays, consider how God has spoken to you in this session. How have you realized God's holiness in new ways? How will that change your relationship with God? How are you being called to be set apart for God? Take some time for silent prayer to tell God what you are thinking and ask Him for help to do as He calls.

▶This Coming Week

1. Fill in the following: My response to God's Holiness this week will be to:

_____

_____

_____

_____

2. Touch base sometime before the next session with your weekly challenge partner to compare notes on how you're both doing with the goals you've set.

3. To learn more about God's Holiness read the section in Bill Bright's *Discover God*, on *God Is Holy*. If you don't have a copy of the book, you can find it online to download and print out for free. Just go to www.DiscoverGod.com.

4. If you'd like to discover and connect with God even more deeply each day throughout the coming week, visit www.DiscoverGod.com.

To discover more about God's Holiness,
start your journey on page 11 of
the Discover God Bible.

BECAUSE GOD IS
LOVE,

He is unconditionally committed to my well-being.

"*Nothing we do will take away His love for us…We need never fear that His blessings are a disguise for other intentions. All God's actions toward us flow out of His pure love for us.*"

—*Bill Bright,* Discover God

▶ For this session, you'll need…

- Three statues or stuffed animals
- A rubber mallet or, if possible, an auction gavel
- A wrapped gift with a real gift inside that a subgroup can share

Sunday school teachers:
If you're using this study for a class rather than a small group, consider starting with the "Dig and Discover" section (beginning on page 33) to help your class stay within its time limits. (If you choose to skip the "Warm Up and Tune In" section, you won't need the statues and stuffed animals.)

▶ Warm Up and Tune In (10 minutes)

Take a few minutes to check in with each other as a group by answering the following question: "If you could describe your past week in just one word, what word would you use, and why?" If some people are new to the group, urge group members to share their names before answering this question.

Once everyone has answered the question, the group can sit in a circle, with one chair in the middle.

Leader: Give the following game instructions to the group. Make sure all group members get to participate, either as part of the guessing team or as the actor.

We're going to play a special kind of Charades. Three to five people will sit in the chairs and guess as a team, while one person serves as the "actor." When the team is seated, I'll bring out a statue or stuffed animal and stand behind the team members so they can't see the object. The actor will act out what he or she sees, but cannot use words or noises. The team then tries to guess what I'm holding. We'll keep going with teams and actors until everyone has had a chance to play.

After the game, gather in a circle and discuss the following questions:

■ What actions helped the team members identify the item they couldn't see?

■ What if I could somehow hold up God behind the guessing team? What are some things the actor could do to get the team to guess correctly God's identity?

■ What if I could somehow hold up love behind the guessing team? What are some things the actor could do to help the team guess "love"?

■ What if I could somehow hold up God's love behind the guessing team? What are some things the actor could do to help the team guess "God's love"?

■ What actions have you observed or taken in the past few weeks that helped someone else "see" or better understand the unseen God? How about helping someone see God's love?

*G*OD IS PERSONAL: Love

God's love isn't just for humanity in general. His immeasurable love is for each of us as individuals as well. Read Matthew 18:12-14 on your own time. Meditate on what the story says about God's love for you, as well as how deeply He wants to be in fellowship with you.

This week, try to look at each person you meet in light of this story.

"*G*od's love is the only reason we exist. It is the why of creation, whereas His power is the how."

—*Bill Bright*, Discover God

▶ Dig and Discover (40 minutes)

- Describe what love is.

- Describe what love is not.

Read 1 John 4:9-10, and then answer the following questions:

- Based on what John writes here, how do you think God would describe authentic love?

- Describe a time you experienced *authentic* love, either from God or another person. How did that experience change your relationship? How did that experience inspire you to show genuine love in your relationships with others?

Have you experienced God's love in your own life? Have you ever thought of His love as the reason you exist? If so, how does that affect your relationship with God? With others?

You really can experience God's love in your life! To learn more, go to www.DiscoverGod.com.

Now, break into subgroups.

Leader: To help increase your group's participation, break into smaller subgroups of three or four. You can ask for volunteers to serve as subgroup leaders, or you can recruit individuals before your class or group meets.

Subgroup leaders: Find a place where your subgroup can strategize without being heard by the other subgroups.

▶ Activity

We're going to have an auction for the wrapped gift in the middle of the room.

Each subgroup must decide what it agrees to give in order to get the gift. For example, you might each make a financial donation of, say, $5 each. Or you might commit to a specific activity as a group: "We will stay and help clean up the room after everyone leaves."

Write down your bids and give them to the leader. When the leader has received all bids, he or she will read them and announce the strongest bid. However, because bids aren't all in dollar values, the strongest bid is up to the leader's subjective judgment.

Now, go back into your subgroup area. Read Ephesians 2:4–9 and discuss the following:

■ Think about the art of gift giving from the perspectives of both the giver and the receiver. What's the responsibility of each person?

■ Why do you think we often try to earn God's love?

■ What does God ask us to sacrifice in order to receive His love?

Based on Ephesians 2:4–9, the leader will now give the gift accordingly.

"The notion of God's love coming to us free of charge, no strings attached, seems to go against every instinct of humanity. The Buddhist eight-fold path, the Hindu doctrine of karma, the Jewish covenant, and Muslim code of law—each of these offers a way to earn approval. Only Christianity dares to make God's love unconditional."

—Philip Yancey, What's So Amazing About Grace?

" *Y*our roots will grow down into God's love and keep you strong. And may you have the power to understand, as all God's people should, how wide, how long, how high, and how deep his love is"

(Ephesians 3:17-18).

Read Romans 8:35–39 in your subgroups, and discuss the following:

■ Describe a time you felt separated from God's love. Did one of the "separators" listed in this passage factor into that feeling? How?

■ In light of the promise of this passage, do you sometimes feel separated from God's love? Why?

■ How does God's faithfulness in the past help you trust in His love today?

" *L*ove is patient and kind. Love is not jealous or boastful or proud or rude. It does not demand its own way. It is not irritable, and it keeps no record of being wronged. It does not rejoice about injustice but rejoices whenever the truth wins out. Love never gives up, never loses faith, is always hopeful, and endures through every circumstance"

(1 Corinthians 13:4-7).

■ Read 1 Corinthians 13:4–7 above, and then look at the list to the right. Does one or more of those words (or others) represent an area in your life right now where you desperately need God's love? How might your life look different if you really embraced God's love for you?

Addiction
Broken relationships
Hopelessness
Jealousy
Critical attitude
Poor self-image
Conflict
Depression
Failure
Bad habits
Unexpected illness
Financial troubles
Stress
Sexual temptations
Unemployment
Anxiety
Transitions
Apathy
Bitterness
Disappointment
Fear
Panic
Suffering
Tension
Dissatisfaction
Vulnerable
Worry
Anger
Hatred
Questioning God
Resentment
Self-centeredness
Trials
Unhappiness

To hear others discuss how they've experienced God's love, go to www.DiscoverGod.com.

Come back together as a larger group, and share any high-lights or questions from your subgroup discussion.

"*The* love of God is one of the great realities of the universe, a pillar upon which the hope of the world rests. But it is a personal, intimate thing, too. God does not love populations, He loves people. He loves not masses, but men. He loves us all with a mighty love that has no beginning and can have no end."

—A. W. Tozer, The Knowledge of the Holy

"*Why* would God stoop to love such unworthy people as we are? Our mortal minds cannot comprehend its vastness or its consistency. We will never be able to answer why, but we can believe it is true, cause us to love, appreciate, worship, and praise Him all the more in return."

—Bill Bright, Discover God

▶ Reflect and Respond (15 minutes)

Loving others isn't a requirement for being loved by God. Rather, it's the outward sign and result of being loved by God. If you have trouble loving God or loving others, perhaps you're not experiencing God's love for you.

Read John 13:34-35. Then discuss the following:

■ Why are we to love others?

■ How do you think we can learn to love like Jesus loved? What's the key?

■ What are some ways you can pass on the gift of God's authentic love to others this week? What, if anything, do you need to "sacrifice" in order to do this (time, money, energy, sleep)?

■ Do you think it's worth that sacrifice? Why or why not?

"*We* who have experienced God's unconditional love are commanded to share that love with others. But how does God express His supernatural love through us?…The secret is letting God use us as His instruments to love others. We begin that process by loving God and serving Him wholeheartedly."

—Bill Bright, Discover God

■ How would experiencing more of God's unconditional love this week allow you to share His love with others?

Sunday school teachers: *If you have time, break your class into pairs and ask them to do the "Making It Real" section that follows. As your class ends, encourage the pairs to pray together for each other. By doing this in class, the extra accountability will help participants follow through on the assignments they choose. Urge the pairs to touch base during the week—as weekly challenge partners—to encourage each other and compare notes.*

If you're out of time, assign this section to your class as homework. It's an opportunity to make God's love come alive in very real and practical ways.

GOD'S CHARACTER IN CONTEXT

Session 2 focused on God's holiness: "Because God is holy, I will devote myself to Him in purity, worship, and service." This session focused on God's love: "Because God is love, He is unconditionally committed to my well-being."

How do you think God can be completely and unconditionally loving without compromising His holiness and purity?

▶ Making It Real (25 minutes)

Break into pairs.

The options below can help you make God's love a part of your *own* life as you put the ideas into practice. Select the option you'd like to take on this week, and share your choice with your partner. Then make plans to connect sometime between now and the next session to check in and encourage each other.

- ☐ **OPTION 1: Write a love letter to God.** In the letter, tell God why you love Him. Be specific! Thank God for His acts of love in your life, take note of how He shows love to those you love, and describe ways you'd like to return that love. When finished, decide on a way to "deliver" the letter: (1) Burn it like an Old Testament sacrifice; (2) send it to another person in your group; (3) put it in a sealed bottle and send it out to sea; or (4) put it away for safekeeping to open and read as a reminder a year from now.

- ☐ **OPTION 2: Show God's love to someone who is down.** Think through the list of calamities in Romans 8:35-39. Do you know anyone who is going through one of those crises right now? Recall what John writes in 1 John 4:12—that people "see" God through our love. Find a way to show love this week to the individual. It should be through a concrete act: giving financial assistance, being physically present at the hospital, helping find a job, or helping in some other practical way.

- ☐ **OPTION 3: Visit those who have sacrificed sons and daughters.** There are people in your community and even in your church who have sacrificed sons and daughters in service to a greater good—people whose children sacrificed their lives in war, on the mission field, or serving closer to home as police officers and firefighters. When you visit these people, find ways to show God's love to them. Afterward, reflect on what you learned from the experience, jot down a few notes, and insert them in your Bible at 1 John 4:10.

☐ **OPTION 4: Make a love journal.** During the coming week make a journal of all the ways God shows His love toward you. Go into each day with an openness to see God's love around you. At the end of the day, write down everything you saw or experienced that communicated God's love. Take time to pray a prayer of thanks for these expressions of love. At the end of the week, read through the journal. How did noting these acts of love each day affect you?

☐ **OPTION 5: Show and tell someone else what God has done for you.** Think of someone you know who really needs to experience a bit of God's love. Think about a small gesture you could make to encourage this person in his or her journey this week. Deliver a small gift of homemade cookies or give him or her a gift certificate to a favorite restaurant. Or shovel the snow off the person's sidewalk or mow the lawn as a gesture of kindness. If you get a chance, talk about a time you meaningfully experienced God's love in your own life.

▶ Prayer

Come back together as a group. What's been weighing on you that you'd appreciate your group praying about? Gather in a circle, and various group members can pray for these shared concerns. After each person prays, the rest of the group should respond in unison with the words, "Thank you, God, for your love!"

"I am the vine; you are the branches. Those who remain in me, and I in them, will produce much fruit. For apart from me you can do nothing"

(John 15:5).

▶ This Coming Week

1. Fill in the following: My response to God's Love this week will be to:

_____

_____

_____

_____

2. Touch base sometime before the next session with your weekly challenge partner to compare notes on how you're both doing with the goals you've set.

3. To learn more about God's holiness read the section in Bill Bright's *Discover God*, on *God Is Love*. If you don't have a copy of the book, you can find it online to download and print out for free. Just go to www.DiscoverGod.com.

4. If you'd like to discover and connect with God even more deeply each day throughout the coming week, visit www.DiscoverGod.com.

To discover more about God's Love,
start your journey on page 545 of
the Discover God Bible.

BECAUSE GOD IS
EVER-PRESENT,
He is always with me.

"We are the result of God's marvelous workmanship.
He designed us. He made our bodies wonderfully complex. He was present
from the moment of conception, is present every moment we live,
and will be present when we die."

—Bill Bright, Discover God

▶ For this session, you'll need...

- A rotary fan

- A candle

- A stack or roll of pennies

- Legal-size blank paper and a pencil for each participant

Sunday school teachers:
If you're using this study for
a class rather than a small
group, consider starting with
the "Dig and Discover" section
(beginning on page 43) to help
your class stay within its time
limits.

▶ Warm Up and Tune In (10 minutes)

Take this opportunity for your group to unwind, relax, and
spend a few minutes getting to know each other a little
better.

Leader: Divide your class or group into "trios"—groups of
three. If the math doesn't work out perfectly, you can have
one or two groups of four people. In that case, three of the
people should be "talkers" in the following activity.

In your group of three, take turns talking about a recent time you wished you could have been in two places at once. Take about a minute for each person to share.

After sharing, designate one person in your trio as the "listener" and the other two as "talkers." At the same time, the two talkers will engage the listener in two separate conversations about two different subjects. The listener will try to listen to both talkers and respond to both simultaneously. You have two minutes for your "double conversation." Go!

When your two minutes are up, return to the larger group and discuss the following questions together:

■ How difficult was it to engage in two separate conversations at the same time? Why?

■ In what ways do you try to multitask like this in your daily life? Does it seem to help? Why or why not?

■ When, in your life, do you wish you could be in two places at once?

GOD IS PERSONAL: Ever-Present

Is God really paying attention to you? Read the first chapter of Jonah on your own time. You'll see what happened when one man tried to run away from God and go where he thought God wouldn't find him.

Just as God had a personal plan for Jonah, God has a personal plan for you, too. How will you respond when God leads you in a specific direction? Let Hebrews 4:13 be a reminder for you to be accountable to God.

▶ Dig and Discover (40 minutes)

■ What does it mean that God is ever-present?

Read Psalm 139:1–12. Then answer the following questions:

■ From these verses, what's your first impression of God's presence in our lives?

■ King David, who wrote this psalm, had a life of ups and downs. One minute, he was the chosen king of Israel, dancing in the streets and praising God. The next minute, he was on his knees, begging God to forgive him for committing adultery and murder. Considering his life, why do you think this psalm was important to David?

■ Why do you think God watches over us at all times?

■ How does it make you feel to know that you're never alone?

Leader: Place the fan, a lit candle, and a stack of pennies on tables in three different corners of the room.

Take a few minutes to go to each table. Close your eyes and let the fan blow on your face. Blow out the candle and see if the room gets darker (then relight the candle for someone else to blow out). Take a few pennies and drop them onto the floor.

These simple items can help us better understand God's constant presence. The fan represents air, the candle represents light, and the pennies represent gravity. Let's talk about how air, light, and gravity are always with us.

■ In what ways are air, light, and gravity ever-present? Can you think of a time one of these elements might not be present? What would happen if we didn't have air? Light? Gravity?

■ How do these elements compare to God's constant presence?

> "*S*ome people see God as a 'great traffic cop' in the sky watching their every move. I like to think that He loves me so much that He cannot take His eyes off me. I am the 'apple of His eye.' Thank You, Father, for watching over us."
>
> —Bill Bright, Discover God

■ Have you experienced God's constant presence in your life in a tangible way—like experiencing air, light, or gravity? If so, what did it look like and how did it affect your relationship with God? Yourself? Others?

You really can experience God's constant presence in your life! To learn more, go to www.DiscoverGod.com.

Now, break into subgroups.

Leader: Break into smaller subgroups to ensure that everyone is involved and engaged with the study. The best size for a subgroup in this session is three, but two or four can also work. You can ask for volunteers to serve as subgroup leaders, or you can recruit individuals before your class or group meets.

Each subgroup will select a Bible passage to explore together from the list on page 45. Depending on the size of your group, some passages might be used by more than one subgroup or some might not be used at all.

Subgroup leaders: Find a place where your subgroup can talk with few distractions. Plan to come back together in 15 minutes.

▶ Activity

Everyone take a sheet of blank legal-size paper and a pencil. Take three or four minutes to draw a timeline of your life from birth to present. Note at least 10 significant events or situations in your life along different points of the timeline.

After a few minutes, share your timeline with the other members of your subgroup. Discuss the following questions:

- Is there a specific moment on your timeline when you remember clearly recognizing God's presence? How did you know God was present in that circumstance?

- Are there any significant situations in your life where you weren't as confident about God's presence? Why or why not?

- Do you think people sometimes don't give God enough credit for His presence? Do you think people sometimes give God too much credit for His presence? Why or why not?

- How can you personally recognize and identify God's presence in your life?

> "*A*ll we have to do is to recognize God as being intimately present within us. Then we may speak directly to Him every time we need to ask for help, to know His will in moments of uncertainty, and to do whatever He wants us to do in a way that pleases Him."
>
> —Brother Lawrence, The Practice of the Presence of God

"*D*o not be afraid or discouraged. For the Lord your God is with you wherever you go"

(Joshua 1:9).

Choose one of the following Bible passages to explore together:

Genesis 3:1-22

Exodus 3:1-6

Exodus 19:16-19

Joshua 1:1-9

Daniel 6:13-23

Jonah 1

Now, discuss the following questions:

- How did God manifest His presence in the passage your subgroup read?

- Why did God need to be present in the situation described in the passage?

- What might have happened if God had not been present in those situations?

Addiction
Broken relationships
Hopelessness
Jealousy
Critical attitude
Poor self-image
Conflict
Depression
Failure
Bad habits
Unexpected illness
Financial troubles
Stress
Sexual temptations
Unemployment
Anxiety
Transitions
Apathy
Bitterness
Disappointment
Fear
Panic
Suffering
Tension
Dissatisfaction
Vulnerable
Worry
Anger
Hatred
Questioning God
Resentment
Self-centeredness
Trials
Unhappiness

■ Look at the list to the left. Does one or more of those words (or others) represent an area in your life right now where you need God's certain and constant presence? How might your life be different if you really embraced God's presence with you at every moment and in every place?

To hear others discuss how they've experienced God's presence, go to www.DiscoverGod.com.

Come back together as a larger group, and take turns sharing highlights from your subgroup discussion.

"*It comforts me to think that if we are created beings, the thing that created us would have to be greater than us, so much greater, in fact, that we would not be able to understand it.*"

—Donald Miller, Blue Like Jazz

▶ Reflect and Respond (15 minutes)

Read Hebrews 13:5 and 1 Peter 5:7. Then discuss the following:

■ Remember how the fan represented the presence of air? When you're overwhelmed by too many things in life, you might feel suffocated—like you can't get enough air. According to these verses, how can God's presence give you a breath of fresh air?

Read 2 Corinthians 4:6, Psalm 119:105, and Ephesians 5:8–9. Then discuss the following:

■ The candle represented the presence of light. You might feel like you're in the dark, groping around with no clear vision or answers. How can God's presence be a light in your darkness?

Read Psalm 32:8 and Proverbs 3:5–6. Then discuss the following:

■ Dropping a stack of pennies represented the presence of gravity. Sometimes your life might feel ungrounded—as if you're left to float around on your own. How can God's presence direct your path and keep your feet on solid ground?

■ If you had been more aware of God's presence in your life during the past few weeks, what would you have done differently?

"He is here with us right now and forever—because He is our ever-present God. He is our guide for life and for eternity. What an incredible truth! What a powerful motivation for us to know, love, trust, obey, worship, and enjoy the presence of our wonderful God and Savior."

—Bill Bright, Discover God

"No person or circumstances can ever remove us from the presence of our loving God."

— Bill Bright, Discover God

■ As a group, how can you help one another recognize and welcome God's presence?

■ If you could personally experience God's presence in your life during the coming week, how would that give you greater hope?

GOD'S CHARACTER IN CONTEXT

Session 3 focused on God's love: "Because God is love, He is unconditionally committed to my well-being." This session focused on God's constant presence: "Because God is ever-present, He is always with me."

How do you think these two attributes of God complement each other? Do you see evidence of God's love and presence in your own life? Explain.

Sunday school teachers: *If you have time, break your class into pairs and ask them to do the "Making It Real" section that follows. As your class ends, encourage the pairs to pray together for each other. By doing this in class, the extra accountability will help participants follow through on the assignments they choose. Urge the pairs to touch base during the week—as weekly challenge partners—to encourage each other and compare notes.*

If you're out of time, assign this section to your class as homework. It's an opportunity to make God's presence come alive in very real and practical ways.

▶ Making It Real (25 minutes)

Break into pairs.

The options below can help you make God's presence a part of your *own* life as you put the ideas into practice. Select the option you'd like to take on this week, and share your choice with your partner. Then make plans to connect sometime between now and the next session to check in and encourage each other.

☐ **OPTION 1: A thank you present.** Consider ways that God has been the "air, light, and gravity" in your life. Write God a thank you letter, showing Him your gratitude for the ways His presence has given you each of those things in the past few weeks. After you write it, read it aloud as a prayer to God. Since God is ever-present, He'll hear—and bask in—every word.

☐ **OPTION 2: Through others' eyes.** Pick up a newspaper or magazine and find one article that portrays some kind of suffering in a person's life and one article that portrays a triumph in a person's life. Take a few minutes to compare these stories to the Bible verses you read in this session. Write down one way you can see God's presence in the person's life in each article.

☐ **OPTION 3: Be present.** Select a significant person in your life—your spouse, a son or daughter, a grandparent, a close friend, or some other person who's important to you. Give that person your complete attention for a full 30 minutes this week. Be present for that person in a way you've never been before, entirely focused on him or her with your eyes, ears, and heart. Set aside all distractions and let that person feel your presence. Then prayerfully consider how God gives you that kind of attention every moment of your life.

☐ **OPTION 4: Don't leave home without it.** Pray for the right attitude, and then ask five non-Christians the following two survey questions: (1) What are the top three things you must have with you at all times? (2) What would happen if you didn't have these items with you? Engage them in a friendly conversation about why certain things are important to bring along. Find a natural point in the discussion where you can talk about the one thing you would never go anywhere without: God. For example, if someone turns the question on you and asks what three things you must have at all times, you can answer that God would be your top choice. Then tell them, in a nonconfrontational way, why God's presence in your life is so important. If possible, illustrate your point with a story from your own experience.

☐ **OPTION 5: Wrap it up.** Find a small box, and ask each family member to write his or her name on a piece of paper and slip it inside. Let everyone have a role in wrapping the gift (make it beautiful!), and then place it in a visible place in your home as a reminder of the gift of God's constant presence in your home. Each day, read one of the Bible passages on page 45. Spend a few minutes talking about whether God still shows His presence in that way today.

" I am the vine; you are the branches. Those who remain in me, and I in them, will produce much fruit. For apart from me you can do nothing"

(John 15:5).

▶ Prayer

Come back together as a group. Share your prayer requests. As the leader prays, be adding your own silent prayers, thanking God for His constant and certain presence in your life.

▶ This Coming Week

1. Fill in the following: My response to God's Constant Presence this week will be to:

_____

_____

_____

_____

2. Touch base sometime before the next session with your weekly challenge partner to compare notes on how you're both doing with the goals you've set.

3. To learn more about God's Constant Presence read the section in Bill Bright's *Discover God*, on *God Is Ever-Present*. If you don't have a copy of the book, you can find it online to download and print out for free. Just go to www.DiscoverGod.com.

4. If you'd like to discover and connect with God even more deeply each day throughout the coming week, visit www.DiscoverGod.com.

To discover more about God's Constant Presence, start your journey on page 368 of the Discover God Bible.

BECAUSE GOD IS
ABSOLUTE TRUTH,
I will believe what He says and live accordingly.

"We must always measure our beliefs by the truth in God's Word. Since He is the author of truth and since absolute truth resides in Him, He is the only One who can guide us to absolute truth. With Him, we see truth face to face."

—*Bill Bright*, Discover God

▶ For this session, you'll need...

■ A compass

■ Enough blank pieces of paper and markers for each person

Sunday school teachers:
If you're using this study for a class rather than a small group, consider starting with the "Dig and Discover" section (beginning on page 55) to help your class stay within its time limits. (If you choose to skip the "Warm Up and Tune In" section, you won't need the compass from the supply list above.)

▶ Warm Up and Tune In (10 minutes)

Take a few minutes to check in with each other as a group by answering the following question: "If you could write a theme song for your past week, what would the title be, and why?" As a bonus, you can sing the song (just kidding). If some people are new to the group, urge group members to share their names before answering this question.

After everyone has answered the question, break up into smaller groups of six or fewer people.

Leader: After the smaller groups have formed, ask group members to stand, leaving several arms'-length of space between each other.

Make sure you have room to move around a bit. Now shut your eyes, raise one arm, and point straight ahead. With your eyes still closed, spin around three times. Without opening your eyes, point in the direction you think is north.

Once all group members have stopped spinning and pointed to what they think is north, all can open their eyes. Chances are, all the arms will be pointed in wildly different directions.

When it seems like the dizziness from the spinning has ended, do the activity again several times. Try the activity without spinning—while a few more people might actually point north, many will still be pointing in various incorrect directions.

Now look at a compass to see which direction is truly north. Once everyone has seen the compass, discuss the following questions:

■ How successful were you at pointing north before seeing the compass?

■ Once you saw north on the compass, how certain were you that north was indeed where the compass pointed?

■ If you weren't familiar with the room or other land-marks, do you think you could ever know for certain which way is north from within yourself?

■ What do you use as your "compass" when you have to make a hard decision?

■ How can the compass serve as a metaphor for God and His truth?

■ Describe a time you had a difficult decision to make and you had no idea what to do? What difference do you think it might have made if you'd been more intentional about making God and His character your "compass"?

GOD IS PERSONAL: Absolute Truth

Each day, we make decisions based on beliefs and values that we assume are true. Later, we might discover that our beliefs were just an illusion of truth projected by our personal desires or the culture. Think about that for a minute. Maybe you gossip with a friend about another friend who isn't present. What's the harm of a little gossip? After all, in our culture, entire TV shows and magazines are devoted to celebrity gossip. However, the Bible cautions against spending time "gossiping from house to house, meddling in other people's business" (1 Timothy 5:13). The world's viewpoint is often based on self-centered values, shortsighted purposes, and ideas that vacillate with the times. However, God's liberating truth serves as our anchor point for life. Read Proverbs 12:19 on your own. Because God's truth lasts for eternity, you can rest assured that God is able to free you from sin each day—even sin that prevents you from turning to Him.

▶ Dig and Discover (40 minutes)

■ What do you think the term *absolute truth* means?

According to a study conducted by The Barna Group, only 22 percent of Americans believe there are "moral absolutes that are unchanging."

■ Why do you think so many people don't believe in any moral absolutes?

■ What do you believe, and why?

■ What do you think the phrase "God is absolute truth" means?

Deuteronomy 32:4 says, "He is the Rock; his deeds are perfect. Everything he does is just and fair. He is a faithful God who does no wrong; how just and upright he is!" As you think about this verse, discuss the following questions:

■ This verse describes God as "the Rock." How does that word picture symbolize God's attribute of absolute truth?

■ Read the verse again. How does each line in the verse further clarify God as absolute truth?

■ If God is absolute truth and you believe in God, what does that mean for your life?

Now read Hosea 4:1–3, and then answer the following questions:

■ According to these verses, what happened to the Israelites when they had no knowledge of God?

■ Because the Israelites had no knowledge of God, they had turned away from truth. What evidence of this do you see in these verses?

■ How would you compare this passage to today's culture?

■ Do you think it's reasonable to believe in absolute truth yet not believe in God? Do you think it's reasonable to believe in the God of the Bible, yet not believe in unchanging truth?

■ What might be some potential pitfalls of not accepting the concept of absolute truth?

Have you truly experienced God's truth in your life? If so, what did it look like and how did it affect your relationship with God? Yourself? Others?

You really can experience God's absolute truth in your life! To learn more, go to www.DiscoverGod.com.

Now, break into subgroups.

Leader: To help increase your group's participation, break into smaller subgroups of four to six. You can ask for volunteers to serve as subgroup leaders, or you can recruit individuals before your class or group meets. As part of this activity, you'll read aloud the following statements, one at a time.

Subgroup leaders: Find a place where your subgroup can talk with few distractions. Plan to come back together in 25 minutes.

▶ Activity

Break your subgroups into pairs, and then give each pair a blank piece of paper and a pen or marker.

Read the following statements to each other. If you agree with the statement, answer "yes" by making a tally mark on your blank paper. Keep track of how many marks you make.

Here are the statements:

- It's always wrong when someone murders an innocent person.
- It's always wrong when a woman is violently raped.
- It's always wrong to censor free speech.
- It's always wrong when the powerful abuse the weak.
- It's always wrong to deliberately damage the environment.
- It's always wrong when someone lies to you in order to manipulate you.
- It's always wrong to steal from an elderly, frail widow living on a meager pension.
- It's always wrong to break the law.
- It's always wrong when someone enslaves an innocent person against his or her will.
- It's always wrong to sexually molest a young child.
- It's always wrong to torture an innocent child.
- It's always wrong to commit a hate crime.
- It's always wrong to discriminate against another person based strictly on the color of his or her skin.

■ It's always wrong for your best friend to sleep with your spouse behind your back.

■ It's always wrong to judge another person.

■ Can you think of anything else that is always wrong? (Make a tally mark for each additional statement you can think of that is always wrong.)

Now look at your tally marks—how many questions did you answer "yes" to?

If you answered "yes" to even one of these questions, then you believe that absolute or unchanging truth exists. The only issue that remains is to determine the source of absolute truth.

Now discuss the following questions in your subgroup:

■ Based on the activity, did your view of absolute truth change? Does that surprise you? Why or why not?

■ Do you agree with the premise of the activity—that to answer "yes" to even one of the questions is to admit the existence of absolute or unchanging truth? Explain your answer.

"Let us hold tightly without wavering to the hope we affirm, for God can be trusted to keep his promise"

(Hebrews 10:23).

■ In Numbers 23:19 the Bible states that God can never lie. What does that imply about the concept of absolute truth?

■ How might the implications of believing in absolute truth change the way you live your life?

"The truth is a snare: you cannot have it, without being caught. You cannot have the truth in such a way that you catch it, but only in such a way that it catches you."

—Søren Kierkegaard

Now read Numbers 23:19, Hebrews 6:18, and 2 Timothy 3:14-16 in your subgroups, and discuss the following questions:

■ The world is full of lies and half-truths, but if you're a believer in the God of the Bible, then, by implication, you've accepted the concept of absolute truth. In light of this, how do you think you can go about determining if something is true or not?

■ How can embracing what the Bible says as truth help you live well?

■ How might living with the knowledge of absolute truth make you "salt and light" in your world?

Read John 14:6 and 18:37, and answer the following:

■ Jesus said He came to testify to the truth. What "truth" do you think He's speaking of?

■ Jesus also said that "no one" can come to God except through Him (Jesus). Do you believe that Jesus was telling the truth, or do you wonder if there are many ways to God (meaning that Jesus was lying)? Why?

If you believe that Jesus is the only way to God—and you've never acknowledged that truth before—ask someone who is already following Jesus to help you take the next step on your journey to discovering who God really is, or go to www.DiscoverGod.com to learn more about your next step!

■ Look at the list to the right. Does one or more of those words (or others) represent an area in your life right now where you need to know that God is absolute truth? How would your attitude change in this situation if you could be completely confident of God's truth?

To hear others discuss how they've experienced God's absolute truth, go to www.DiscoverGod.com.

Addiction
Broken relationships
Hopelessness
Jealousy
Critical attitude
Poor self-image
Conflict
Depression
Failure
Bad habits
Unexpected illness
Financial troubles
Stress
Sexual temptations
Unemployment
Anxiety
Transitions
Apathy
Bitterness
Disappointment
Fear
Panic
Suffering
Tension
Dissatisfaction
Vulnerable
Worry
Anger
Hatred
Questioning God
Resentment
Self-centeredness
Trials
Unhappiness

Come back together as a larger group, and share any highlights or questions from your subgroup discussion.

"*G*od's truth frees us to live as God has intended. On the other hand, the Deceiver wants us to base our lives on false assumptions. Jesus said to His followers, 'You are truly My disciples if you keep obeying My teachings. And you will know the truth, and the truth will set you free.' "

—Bill Bright, Discover God

▶ Reflect and Respond (15 minutes)

Read John 10:27-28, Romans 6:22, and Jeremiah 29:11. Then discuss the following:

■ What do you think it means that we can be set free? What messages do we sometimes hear from the world that promise freedom? What do those promises usually deliver?

■ According to these Bible passages, what promises does God offer us that deliver real freedom? If these promises are not absolute truth, then how reliable are they? What are the implications for us if these promises are absolutely true?

■ What's one absolute truth you can choose to embrace this week to help you understand God better? How can this group help you be more assured of God's absolute truth?

■ How would understanding more about God's absolute truth give you hope this week?

Sunday school teachers: *If you have time, break your class into pairs and ask them to do the "Making It Real" section that follows. As your class ends, encourage the pairs to pray together for each other. By doing this in class, the extra accountability will help participants follow through on the assignments they choose. Urge the pairs to touch base during the week—as weekly challenge partners—to encourage each other and compare notes.*

If you're out of time, assign this section to your class as homework. It's an opportunity to make God's truth come alive in very real and practical ways.

GOD'S CHARACTER IN CONTEXT

Session 4 focused on God's constant presence: "Because God is ever-present, He is always with me." This session focused on God's absolute truth: "Because God is absolute truth, I will believe what He says and live accordingly."

How do you think these two attributes of God complement each other? Knowing that God is always present, what evidence of His truth do you see in your life? Explain.

▶ Making It Real (25 minutes)

Break into pairs.

The options below can help you make God's absolute truth a part of your *own* life as you put the ideas into practice. Select the option you'd like to take on this week, and share your choice with your partner. Then make plans to connect sometime between now and the next session to check in and encourage one another.

☐ **OPTION 1: Commit the truth to memory.** Psalm 119:11 says, "I have hidden your word in my heart." Verse 105 says, "Your word is a lamp to guide my feet and a light for my path." Commit to memorizing John 8:31-32 and John 18:37 this week. Hide these verses in your heart, and let them guide you.

☐ **OPTION 2: Spy the lies.** As you watch TV, listen to the radio, or read a printed or electronic news source this week, try to capture three "non-truths" the world tries to feed you (for help, refer to the section "What Is Absolute Truth" in *Discover God* by Bill Bright). Write down these lies, and then find three Bible verses or passages that expose those lies with God's truth. Check in with someone from your group to share your findings, and pray together, thanking God for giving you the absolute truth about the issues.

☐ **OPTION 3: Be free indeed.** If you accept that God's truth really does set you free, take Him at His word. Pray that God will show you one thing to "let go" from your life—that one thing that you've kept a tight grip on and is keeping you from a fully open and free relationship with God. Every day this week, meditate for at least five minutes on Ephesians 4:21-24. Let God speak the truth to you through the promise of His word.

☐ **OPTION 4: True neighbors.** With members of your family or roommates or several neighbors, draw a map of your neighborhood—perhaps the 10 or 20 houses or apartments closest to yours. Introduce yourselves to these neighbors, and tell them you are putting together a map with first names and an interesting fact about each household. Explain that the purpose of your project is to build trust among your neighbors by sharing a little bit of the truth about each other. If the conversation allows, share how knowing the truth about God enables you to trust Him in every part of your life.

☐ **OPTION 5: The truth of the matter.** Think of one "insurmountable" problem you're facing in your life—something you've struggled finding a solution to. Identify the general topic or category associated with that problem, and then do a mini Bible study on that topic. Use a concordance or an oline concordance like biblegateway.com and search for three to five truths in the Bible about your topic. Then pray that God will help you understand how those truths can help you deal with your problem.

▶ Prayer

Come back together as a group. Share your prayer requests. Before your group spends time praying, take a few moments to be silent and appreciate that God *is* absolute truth and that He wants to use His truth to set you free.

"*I* am the vine; you are the branches. Those who remain in me, and I in them, will produce much fruit. For apart from me you can do nothing"

(John 15:5).

▶ This Coming Week

1. Fill in the following: My response to God's Absolute Truth this week will be to:

_____

_____

_____

_____

2. Touch base sometime before the next session with your weekly challenge partner to compare notes on how you're both doing with the goals you've set.

3. To learn more about God's Absolute Truth read the section in Bill Bright's *Discover God*, on *God Is Absolute Truth*. If you don't have a copy of the book, you can find it online to download and print out for free. Just go to www.DiscoverGod.com.

4. If you'd like to discover and connect with God even more deeply each day throughout the coming week, visit www.DiscoverGod.com.

To discover more about God's Absolute Truth, start your journey on page 100 of the Discover God Bible.

BECAUSE GOD IS
MERCIFUL,

He forgives me of my sins when I sincerely confess them.

"God's mercy enables us to break from the habits of sin that have bound us. As a result, we can have peace, joy, fulfillment and purpose."

—*Bill Bright*, Discover God

▶ For this session, you'll need...

■ Five pennies, three blank pieces of paper, and a pencil for each group member

Sunday school teachers:
If you're using this study for a class rather than a small group, consider starting with the "Dig and Discover" section (beginning on page 67) to help your class stay within its time limits. (If you choose to skip the "Warm Up and Tune In" section, you won't need the items in the supply list above.)

▶ Warm Up and Tune In (10 minutes)

If there are any new people in the group, all group members should introduce themselves by giving their name, the names of their family members, and what they are most involved in during the week.

Then, everyone can sit in a circle.

Leader: Give five pennies, three blank pieces of paper, and a pencil to each group member.

Starting with the person in the group with the earliest birthday, and going clockwise from there, share one thing you've done in your life that you think most of the other people in the group have *not* done. Each time a person shares, everyone who has not done that thing must give that person a penny. If you run out of pennies, write the person an IOU. If you have time, go around the group twice. Those in debt at the end of the activity need to get a glass of refreshing ice water for those with the most pennies! The group can then discuss the following:

■ How did it feel to be a debtor, even though this was just a game? How is this different from being a debtor in real life?

■ How does it feel to be one of the people with the most pennies and to have someone else perform an act of service toward you?

■ How does unequal status (debtors versus creditors) affect group dynamics?

■ Why is it hard to owe friends or family money? How does the debt change your relationship?

GOD IS PERSONAL: Mercy

We can speak of God's mercy in an academic way, but we really don't completely understand and appreciate His mercy until it's personal—until we experience it in relation to our own life and our own "indebtedness." Read how Paul felt about the mercy shown to him by God in 1 Timothy 1:15-16. Thank God each day this week for the mercy He's shown to you—a way he's released you from "indebtedness."

▶ Dig and Discover (40 minutes)

■ What comes to mind when you think of God as merciful?

Read Matthew 18:21-35. Then answer the following questions:

■ If you were in Peter's position, how would you have reacted to Jesus' answer to his question about forgiving others? What was Jesus trying to tell Peter about the nature of forgiveness?

■ How does Jesus' parable further explain what He meant in His answer to Peter's question?

■ What's the significance of the difference in amounts, between what this debtor owed the king and what the man's own debtor owed him? What does this say about how God forgives us?

■ Why do you think the king's act of mercy didn't inspire a similar attitude in this man toward his own debtor?

■ When have you found yourself acting like this unforgiving debtor? In such a situation, who or what reminds you of God's mercy toward you?

■ Have you truly experienced God's mercy in your life? If so, what did it look like and how did it affect your relationship with God? Yourself? Others?

" Our merciful God always seeks the welfare, both temporal (life on earth) and eternal (life in heaven forever), of His children and those who have not yet accepted His love and forgiveness. Although many people show mercy to others, God is the grand master of mercy. His very nature desires to relieve us of the self-imposed misery and distress we experience because of our sin."

—Bill Bright, Discover God

You really can experience God's mercy in your life! To learn more, go to www.DiscoverGod.com.

Now, break into subgroups.

Leader: To help increase your group's participation, break into smaller subgroups of three or four. You can ask for volunteers to serve as subgroup leaders, or you can recruit individuals before your class or group meets. **Note:** If performing the following activity is too difficult for someone because of physical limitations, he or she can still participate by being an observer. Observers can share what they see in the reactions of participants.

Subgroup leaders: Find a place where your subgroup can talk with few distractions. Plan to come back together in 25 minutes.

▶ Activity

Break your subgroup into pairs. For each pair, the shortest person should get down on the ground on all fours while the other person stands beside him or her. Make sure each pair is near a wall so the standing person can use it to maintain balance. The standing person should take off his or her shoes and then place one foot on his or her partner's back, squarely between the person's shoulder blades. The standing person should then push the other person down toward the ground. The person on all fours shouldn't resist but should go down as the person pushes him or her down. The standing person should *not* push his or her partner all the way to the floor. Then the standing person should lift his or her foot back up again, and the partner can raise back up. For about one minute, the standing person should control how high or how low the other person can go. Then reverse roles!

After all persons have taken both roles, discuss the following:

■ What were some of the feelings you had when you were on all fours and your partner was pushing you down? What were some of the feelings you had when you were in the standing position?

■ How was this situation similar to creditor/debtor relationships?

■ What do you think motivates a person in a position of dominance to try to "push someone else down"?

■ Have you ever had an experience in your life that this exercise reminded you of? Describe that situation—which position were you in? How did you get out of it?

■ How does fully experiencing God's mercy make it less likely we'll "push someone else down" when we're in a position to do so?

"God is so rich in mercy, and he loved us so much, that even though we were dead because of our sins, he gave us life when he raised Christ from the dead"

(Ephesians 2:4-5).

"To receive mercy we must first know that God is merciful. And it is not enough to believe that He once showed mercy to Noah or Abraham or David and will again show mercy in some happy future day. We must believe that God's mercy is boundless, free and, through Jesus Christ our Lord, available to us now in our present situation."

—A. W. Tozer, The Knowledge of the Holy

Now read Romans 2:4 in your subgroups, and discuss the following questions:

■ Does being merciful toward others make it more likely that they'll change for the better or more likely that they'll become complacent with their sin? What have you experienced that causes you to answer the way you did?

■ This verse describes God as "kind, tolerant, and patient." Tolerance often gets a bad rap these days. How do you think the word "tolerant" relates to God's mercy? How are tolerance and mercy similar? Different?

■ Has God's kindness ever turned you away from sin? Describe how that happened.

Addiction
Broken relationships
Hopelessness
Jealousy
Critical attitude
Poor self-image
Conflict
Depression
Failure
Bad habits
Unexpected illness
Financial troubles
Stress
Sexual temptations
Unemployment
Anxiety
Transitions
Apathy
Bitterness
Disappointment
Fear
Panic
Suffering
Tension
Dissatisfaction
Vulnerable
Worry
Anger
Hatred
Questioning God
Resentment
Self-centeredness
Trials
Unhappiness

■ Look at the list to the left. Does one or more of those words (or others) represent an area in your life right now where you need to experience God's mercy? How might your life look different if you really embraced God's mercy toward you?

To hear others discuss how they've experienced God's mercy, go to www.DiscoverGod.com.

Come back together as a larger group, and share any highlights or questions from your subgroup discussion.

"*The* cross is nobody's private property, but belongs to all; it is intended for all mankind. God loves our enemies—the cross tells us that…God gave the beloved Son for them. That is the whole point every time we encounter enemies we remember at once: God loves them, God gave everything for them…With respect to our attitude toward our enemies, this means first, remember that you were God's enemy and that, without having earned it or being worthy of it, you were met with mercy."

—Dietrich Bonhoeffer, "Christ's Love and Our Enemies," in A Testament to Freedom: The Essential Writings of Dietrich Bonhoeffer

"*God* extended His mercy to us even before we were born, and before we acknowledged our need for His forgiveness. Without our Lord's sacrifice on the cross, we could not have a relationship with God. Now because of Christ's willingness to die in our place, we can have a deep intimacy with the God who loves us unconditionally."

—Bill Bright, Discover God

▶ Reflect and Respond (15 minutes)

Read Hebrews 4:14–16. Then discuss the following:

■ How does Jesus enable us to go to God and boldly believe that he will show mercy and forgive us?

■ Think of a time in your own life when you needed God's mercy and grace the most. What helped you be aware of and accept His mercy and grace at that time?

■ When you begin to have doubts that God will be merciful toward you, what helps you find reassurance?

" *R*emember, people all around you need to be pointed to the mercy of God. Their hearts ache for that unconditional love and complete forgiveness. As ambassadors of Christ, we know the comfort of God's mercy and can show others how to receive this unlimited gift."

—Bill Bright, Discover God

■ If you could really experience God's mercy in your life this week, how would that give you greater hope?

GOD'S CHARACTER IN CONTEXT

Session 5 focused on God's absolute truth: "Because God is absolute truth, I will believe what He says and live accordingly." This session focused on God's mercy: "Because God is merciful, He forgives me of my sins when I sincerely confess them."

How do you think God can offer mercy and forgiveness yet still expect that we'll live according to His absolute truth?

Sunday school teachers: *If you have time, break your class into pairs and ask them to do the "Making It Real" section that follows. As your class ends, encourage the pairs to pray together for each other. By doing this in class, the extra accountability will help participants follow through on the assignments they choose. Urge the pairs to touch base during the week—as weekly challenge partners—to encourage each other and compare notes.*

If you're out of time, assign this section to your class as homework. It's an opportunity to make God's mercy come alive in very real and practical ways.

▶ **Making It Real** (25 minutes)

Break into pairs.

The options below can help you make God's mercy a part of your *own* life as you put the ideas into practice. Select the option you'd like to take on this week, and share your choice with your partner. Then make plans to connect sometime between now and the next session to check in and encourage each other.

☐ **OPTION 1: Your spiritual credit report.** A lot of people today can ask to see your financial credit report, and many people make an effort to keep track of what their own credit report looks like. But what about your *spiritual* credit report—the list that details just how indebted you are to God's mercy? For just one week, make a list of all the times you fall short of what God calls you to do and, because of that, need to rely on God's merciful forgiveness. At the end of each day, go over what happened in that day and add to your list. Then, take a red pen and go over the list again, and across each act on the list, write the word "forgiven!" in red. Then say a prayer of thanks to God for His abundant mercy.

☐ **OPTION 2: Forgive a hard-to-forgive person.** Sometimes it's relatively easy to forgive: The person we're forgiving has forgiven us before, and we know he or she is basically a good person. But most of us also know people we have had a hard time forgiving. We've had angry and bitter feelings toward that person for a long time. Find a person for whom that is true for you. Remembering all that God has forgiven you in Christ, do something to convey your forgiveness to that individual. You might want to make a phone call or write a letter. Or you can simply perform a gesture of good will—maybe doing an unexpected favor or buying the person a cup of coffee. Spend some time in prayer before doing this, to make sure your heart is prepared.

☐ **OPTION 3: Interview a recipient of mercy.** Find a person who has particularly benefited from an act of mercy. Maybe it's a man who committed a crime but had his sentence commuted or was put on parole. Maybe it's a wife who was unfaithful to her husband, but he has taken her back and is genuinely trying to save the marriage. Or maybe this person actually had a financial debt forgiven. While being very careful to respect the person's confidentiality and the sensitivity of the issues involved, explore how this act of mercy has affected his or her life. In what way is that person's story like your own? What can you learn from his or her experience? If you share any of this with your partner, make absolutely sure that you do not share the details of the person's story, unless he or she has given you permission to do so.

☐ **OPTION 4: Have a family night discussion on mercy.** This might be a particularly good choice if you have children in the home. Get together for a half-hour family devotional time focused on mercy. Begin by talking about what mercy is. Focus on what extending mercy to others looks like. Then read a portion of the Bible from elsewhere in this session, or read one of the following: Psalm 145:9; Isaiah 49:13; Daniel 9:9; Micah 6:8; Matthew 5:7; Romans 2:4; or Ephesians 2:4-5. Talk about what the passage you've read says about God's mercy to us. These questions might help your discussion: What can we learn about God's mercy from this passage? What does the passage say about our need to be merciful to others? When have you seen someone being *un*merciful to others (teasing, gossiping, harassing someone who has made a mistake or who does not fit in)? How can you counter such behavior and show the mercy of God in their lives? Ask God for a spirit of mercy in how you relate to people during the week.

☐ **OPTION 5: Have a home meeting on mercy.** Invite both Christian and non-Christian friends to your home. You might want to start the evening by playing a secular song such as "Mercy Now" by Mary Gauthier. Ahead of time, ask for four or five people to share how God has shown mercy in their lives. After these people share, see if others want to do the same. Then ask if anyone wants to talk about his or her own *need* for mercy. Make sure you listen carefully to what each person has to say. Discourage others from giving quick answers to these expressions of need. Consider setting up a time later to talk about how God shows us mercy in Jesus Christ.

▶ Prayer

Come back together as a group. Share your prayer requests. Include people you know who have been victimized by unmerciful behavior. Close your prayer time by gathering in pairs; pray for God's mercy for your partner in all that happens during the week ahead.

"I am the vine; you are the branches. Those who remain in me, and I in them, will produce much fruit. For apart from me you can do nothing"

(John 15:5).

▶ This Coming Week

1. Fill in the following: My response to God's Mercy this week will be to:

_____

_____

_____

_____

2. Touch base sometime before the next session with your weekly challenge partner to compare notes on how you're both doing with the goals you've set.

3. To learn more about God's mercy read the section in Bill Bright's *Discover God*, on *God Is Merciful*. If you don't have a copy of the book, you can find it online to download and print out for free. Just go to www.DiscoverGod.com.

4. If you'd like to discover and connect with God even more deeply each day throughout the coming week, visit www.DiscoverGod.com.

To discover more about God's Mercy,
start your journey on page 13 of
the Discover God Bible.

For more **amazing resources**

visit us at
www.group.com...

...or call us at
1-800-747-6060 ext. 1370!